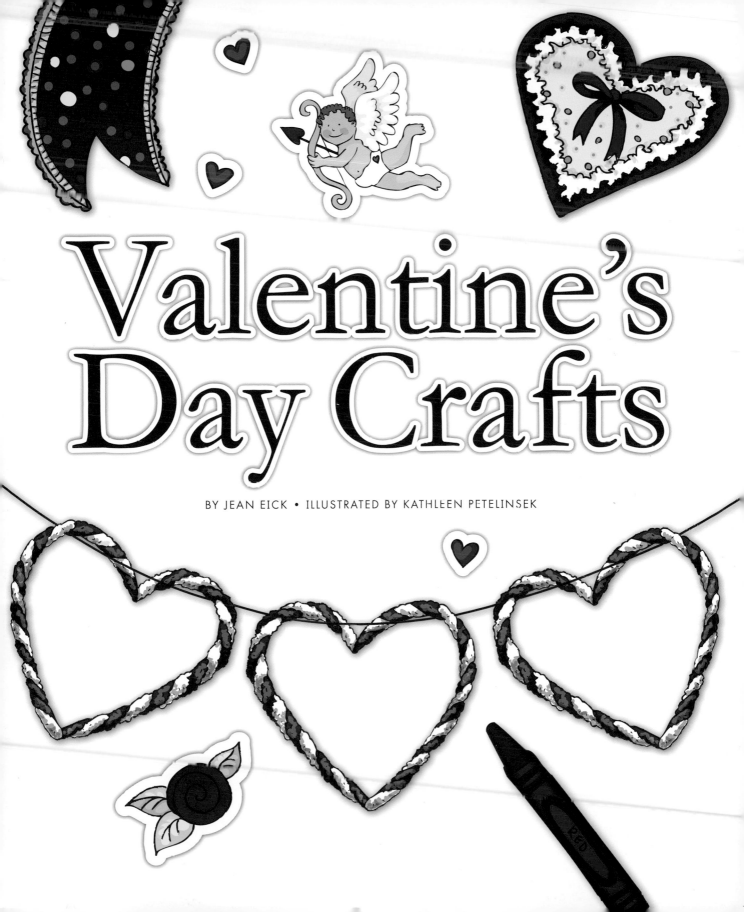

Valentine's Day Crafts

BY JEAN EICK • ILLUSTRATED BY KATHLEEN PETELINSEK

The Child's World

Published by The Child's World®
1980 Lookout Drive
Mankato, MN 56003-1705
800-599-READ
www.childsworld.com

The Child's World®: Mary Berendes, Publishing Director
The Design Lab: Design and production

Library of Congress Cataloging-in-Publication Data
Eick, Jean, 1947–
  Valentine's Day crafts / by Jean Eick; illustrated by Kathleen Petelinsek.
    p. cm.
  ISBN 978-1-60954-279-5 (library bound: alk. paper)
  1. Valentine decorations—Juvenile literature. 2. Handicraft—Juvenile
literature. I. Petelinsek, Kathleen, ill. II. Title.
  TT900.V34E332 2011
  745.594'1—dc22   2010035476

Printed in the United States of America
Mankato, MN
December, 2010
PA02071

Table of Contents

Happy Valentine's Day!

Valentine's Day is a very special **holiday**. It's a time for people to show how much they care for one another. It's also a time to be thankful for the people you love. Valentine's Day has been celebrated for over 600 years.

Valentine's Day is celebrated all over the world. In the United States, Valentine's Day is always on February 14. Some people give candies or flowers to the people they love. Others make homemade gifts to show their feelings. Valentine's Day is a wonderful, fun holiday!

Let's Begin!

1 This book is full of great ideas you can make to celebrate Valentine's Day. There are ideas for decorations, gifts, and cards. There are activities at the end of this book, too!

2 Before you start making any craft, be sure to read the **dircctions**. Make sure you look at the pictures too—they will help you understand what to do. Go through the list of things you'll need and get everything together. When you're ready, find a good place to work. Now you can begin making your crafts!

Pipe-cleaner Hearts

These hearts are quick to make. You can hang them
in sunny windows or even on doorknobs!

THINGS YOU'LL NEED

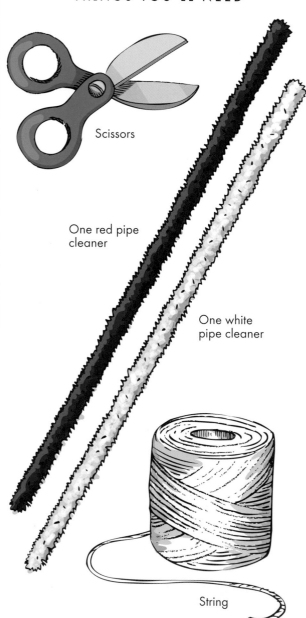

Scissors

One red pipe
cleaner

One white
pipe cleaner

String

DIRECTIONS

1 Put the pipe cleaners side by side.
Starting at one end, twist them together.

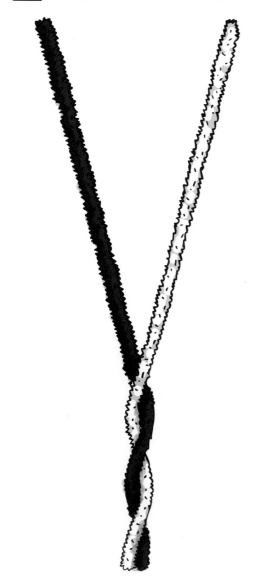

2 Do not twist too tightly—just firm enough to create a nice and even spiral shape.

3 Bend the twisted pipe cleaners into a heart shape.

4 Use some string to hang your heart for everyone to see. You can even put lots of hearts on a long string to go around the room.

Paper Hearts

You can make lots of hearts in different sizes
for decorating walls, doors, and windows.

THINGS YOU'LL NEED

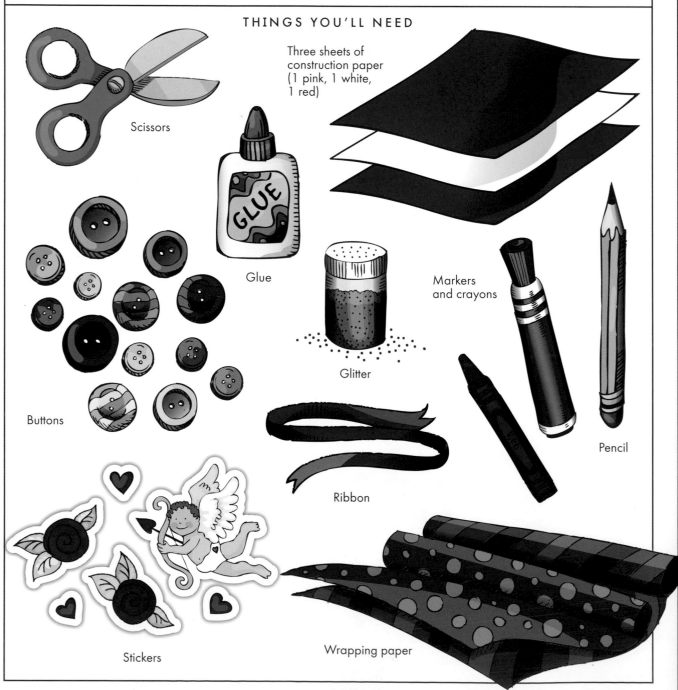

Scissors

Three sheets of
construction paper
(1 pink, 1 white,
1 red)

Glue

Buttons

Glitter

Markers
and crayons

Pencil

Ribbon

Stickers

Wrapping paper

DIRECTIONS

1 Fold a piece of paper in half.

2 Use your pencil to draw half of a heart shape.

3 Carefully cut along the line. When you open the paper, there will be a full heart shape.

4 Decorate the heart however you'd like. You can make hearts in many different ways. Here are some ideas: Use wrapping paper to make a smaller heart than the big one you just made. Glue the wrapping-paper heart to the middle of your large heart.

5 Use crayons and markers to write messages on your hearts. Good ideas are "I love you," and "You're sweet."

Heart Flowers

These sweet flowers are almost as pretty as real flowers!

THINGS YOU'LL NEED

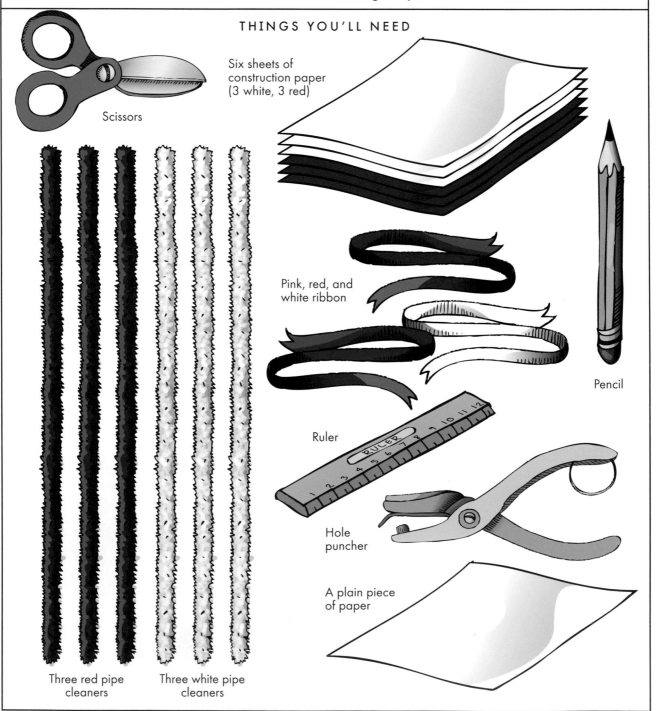

Scissors

Six sheets of
construction paper
(3 white, 3 red)

Pink, red, and
white ribbon

Pencil

Ruler

Hole
puncher

A plain piece
of paper

Three red pipe
cleaners

Three white pipe
cleaners

1 Make a heart from the plain piece of paper. Use the directions from page 11. Carefully cut it out.

2 Use this plain heart to trace three hearts on the red construction paper, and three hearts on the white construction paper.

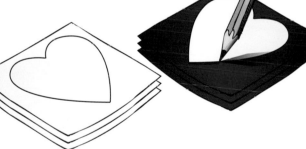

3 Cut out all six hearts.

4 Punch a hole at the top of each heart.

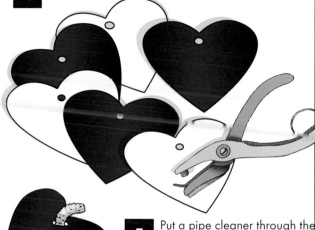

5 Put a pipe cleaner through the hole. Bend the top around so the edge is under the heart.

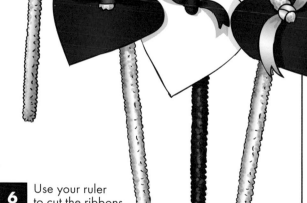

6 Use your ruler to cut the ribbons so each piece is 6 inches long. Tie a ribbon around each pipe cleaner.

Heart Treasures

These tasty presents are as fun to make as they are to give!

THINGS YOU'LL NEED

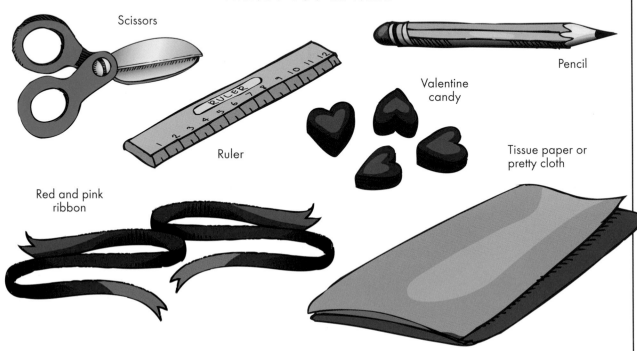

Scissors

Ruler

Valentine candy

Pencil

Tissue paper or pretty cloth

Red and pink ribbon

DIRECTIONS

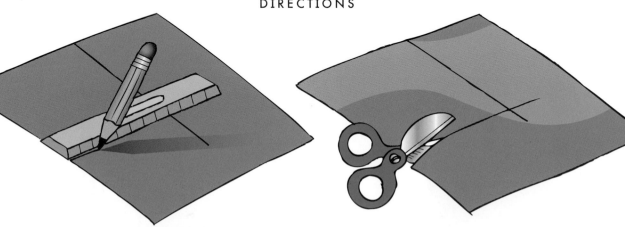

1 Use your pencil and ruler to draw a square on the tissue paper (or cloth). The square should be 8 inches long on each side.

2 Carefully cut out the square.

3 Use your ruler to cut a piece of ribbon that is 12 inches long. Set this **aside**.

4 Put a small **amount** of the candies in the middle of the square.

5 Fold the corners up so they all touch each other.

6 Tie the treasure shut with your piece of ribbon.

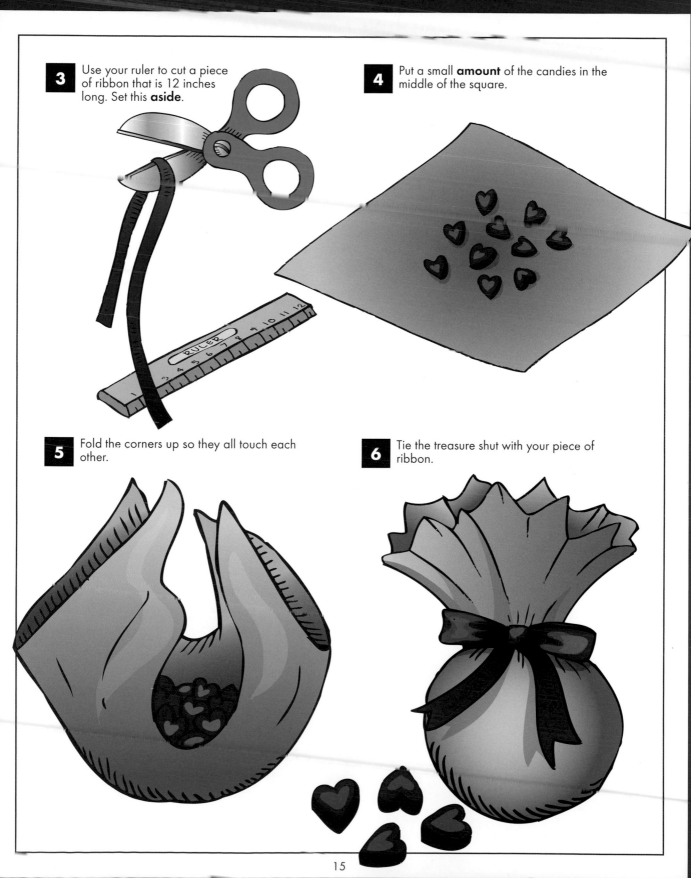

Heart Bookmark

This is an easy gift you can make for your family and friends.

THINGS YOU'LL NEED

Scissors

Ruler

Glue

Pencil

Wide ribbons

Red construction paper

DIRECTIONS

1 Lay the ribbon flat.

2 Fold the paper in half. Lay it over the ribbon.

3 Cut off any extra paper so that the paper and the ribbon are the same **width**.

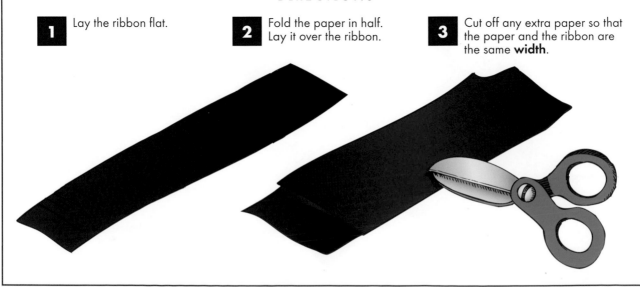

4 Use your pencil to make a half-heart shape on the paper.

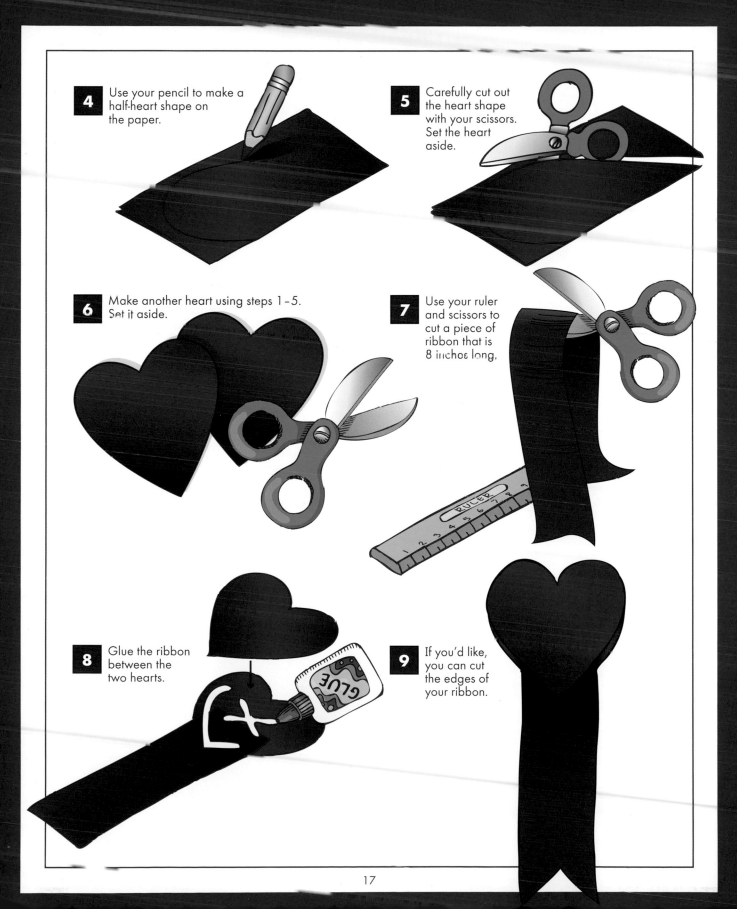

5 Carefully cut out the heart shape with your scissors. Set the heart aside.

6 Make another heart using steps 1–5. Set it aside.

7 Use your ruler and scissors to cut a piece of ribbon that is 8 inches long.

RULER

8 Glue the ribbon between the two hearts.

GLUE

9 If you'd like, you can cut the edges of your ribbon.

Valentine's Day Cards

Everyone likes to get Valentine's Day cards. Making them with your friends can be fun!

THINGS YOU'LL NEED

Scissors

Construction paper (lots of different colors)

Glitter

Glue

Ribbon

Buttons

Pencil

Crayons, markers, or paint

Stickers or magazine pictures

DIRECTIONS FOR CARD ONE

1 Fold a piece of construction paper to the size you want it to be. Folding once will make a large card. Folding it twice will make a smaller card.

2 Decorate the front of the card any way you'd like. You can use ribbons, buttons, glitter, and stickers—be creative! Write a message on the inside of the card. You can decorate the inside, too. Don't forget to sign your name!

DIRECTIONS FOR CARD TWO

1 Instead of making a square card, make one shaped like a heart! Use your pencil to draw a heart shape on a folded piece of paper. Remember, the edge of the heart must hang over the folded part of the paper!

2 Cut out the shape with your scissors.

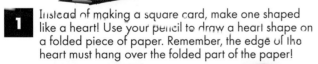

3 Now open the card. You should see two hearts!

4 Decorate the card however you'd like. You can glue pictures of yourself inside, or use pictures from magazines that remind you of Valentine's Day. Some ideas are candies, small hearts, and people hugging.

Envelopes

You can make your own envelopes to fit your homemade cards.

THINGS YOU'LL NEED

Scissors

Pencil

Construction paper, wrapping paper, or a paper bag.

Tape or glue

Ruler

DIRECTIONS TO MAKE A SQUARE ENVELOPE

1 Cut out the front of a plain paper bag.

2 Use your ruler and pencil to mark a square that is 8 inches long on each side. This will be big enough for a 5 ¼-inch card. Mark an "x" in the center of your square (4 inches in from each side).

3 Fold three of the corners so they cover the "x." Tape or glue the corners so they'll stay in place.

4 Place your card inside. Fold the top down and tape it shut.

DIRECTIONS TO MAKE AN ENVELOPE THAT'S NOT SQUARE

1 Use your ruler and pencil to mark a square on a large piece of construction paper or wrapping paper. The paper must be 4 inches taller and 5 inches wider than your card. Draw a line 2 inches down from the top.

2 Fold the top down along the line.

3 Place your card under this flap.

4 Fold in each side over your card.

5 Fold up the bottom.

6 Now take your card out of the envelope.

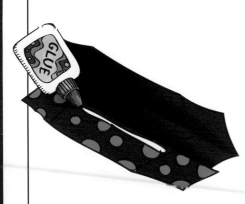

7 Glue the sides of your envelope together. Don't glue the top, however! You have to be able to put your card back inside!

8 Fold up the bottom and glue it in place.

9 Put your card back inside. Fold down the top flap and tape the envelope shut.

Activities

There are many things you can do with others to celebrate Valentine's Day. Here are some fun ideas.

1 Invite your friends over to make cards for all of your classmates. Have each friend bring something for decorating the cards (such as glitter, stickers, or buttons).

2 Have a cookie- or cupcake-decorating party! Ask each person to bring something for decorating (such as frosting, candies, or sprinkles).

3 Have a Valentine's Day pizza party. Decorate a room with white **streamers** and some of the decorations from this book. You can play games and make Valentines for each other.

Glossary

amount (uh-MOWNT) An amount is how much of something there is.

aside (uh-SYD) When something is set aside, it is put somewhere out of the way.

directions (dir-EK-shunz) Directions are the steps for how to do something. You should follow the directions in this book to make your crafts.

holiday (HOL-uh-day) A holiday is a time for celebration, such as Christmas or Mother's Day. Valentine's Day is a holiday.

steamers (STREE-murz) Streamers are long strips of colorful paper or plastic. They are used as decorations.

width (WIDTH) An object's width is how wide it is.

Find More Crafts

BOOKS

Ross, Kathy, and Barbara Leonard (illustrator). *All New Crafts For Valentine's Day*. Brookfield, CT: Millbrook Press, 2002.

Stamper, Judith, Bari Weissman (illustrator), and T.R. Garcia (illustrator). *Valentine Fun Activity Book*. Mahwah, NJ: Troll, 1997.

WEB SITES

Visit our Web site for links to more crafts: childsworld.com/links

Note to Parents, Teachers, and Librarians: We routinely verify our Web links to make sure they are safe and active sites. So encourage your readers to check them out!

Index

ABOUT THE AUTHOR

Jean Eick has written over 200 books for children over the past forty years. She has written biographies, craft books, and many titles on nature and science. Jean lives in Lake Tahoe with her husband and enjoys hiking in the mountains, reading, and doing volunteer work.